Let's Make a Circle Graph

by Robin Nelson

first step nonfiction

Lerner Publications Company · Minneapolis

Mr. Hall wants to make a **circle graph**.

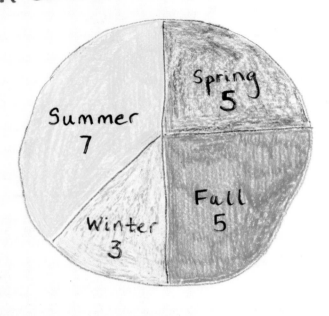

Which Season People Like Best

Spring 5

Summer 7

Fall 5

Winter 3

A circle graph shows parts of a whole.

Mr. Hall **surveys** the class.
He asks a question.

He asks his students how
they get to school.

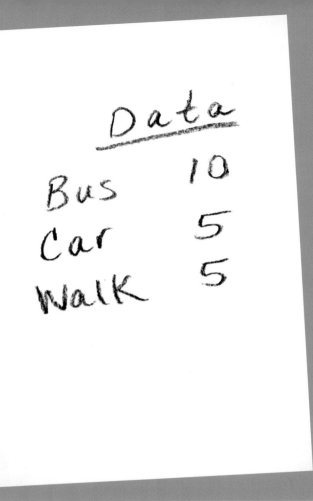

Data

Bus	10
Car	5
Walk	5

The answers are his **data**.

Mr. Hall's class has 20 students.

Mr. Hall draws a circle.

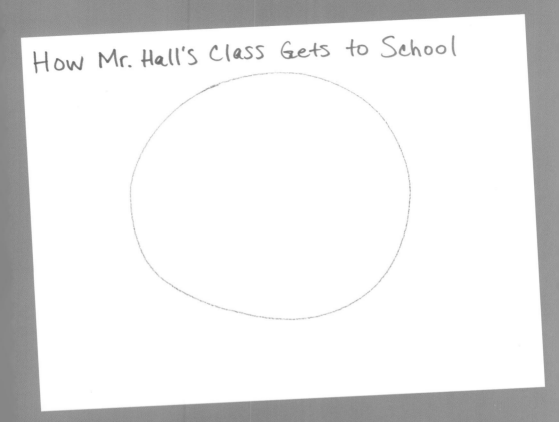

How Mr. Hall's Class Gets to School

The circle stands for the whole class.

Ten kids ride the bus. Ten is one-half of the class.

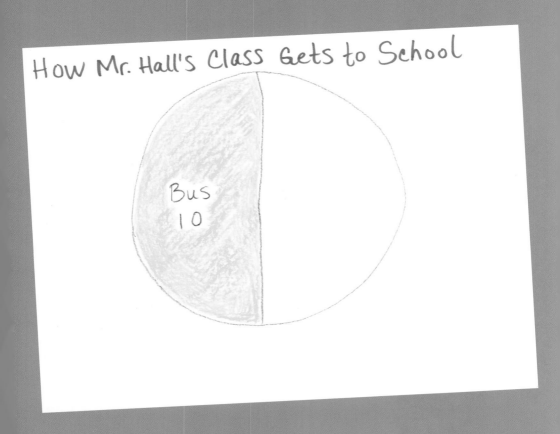

How Mr. Hall's Class Gets to School

Bus
10

Mr. Hall colors half of the circle yellow for bus riders.

Five kids come to school in a car.

Five kids walk to school.

How Mr. Hall's class Gets to School

Bus
10

Five is one-fourth of 20.

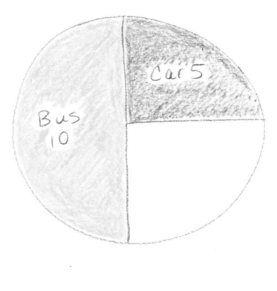

How Mr. Hall's Class Gets to School

Cars

Bus
10

Mr. Hall colors one-fourth of the circle blue for car riders.

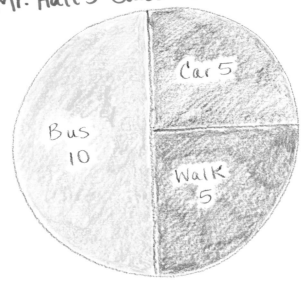

How Mr. Hall's Class Gets to School

Car 5

Bus 10

Walk 5

Mr. Hall colors one fourth of the circle green for walkers.

How Mr. Hall's Class Gets to School

Car 5

Walk 5

Mr. Hall shares the circle graph with his class.

How Mr. Hall's Class Gets to School

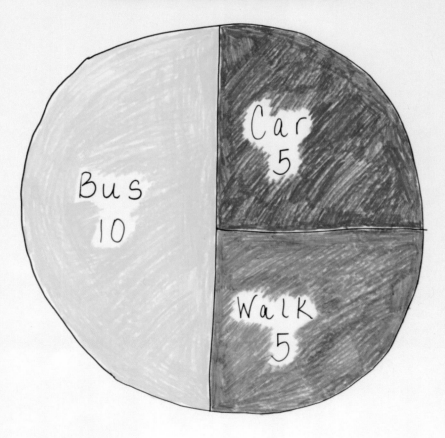

Using a Circle Graph

Use Mr. Hall's graph to answer these questions.

How do most students get to school?

Do more students ride the bus or ride in a car?

Do more students ride in a car or walk?

How much of the whole circle ride the bus?

Facts about Circle Graphs

 A circle graph is made with a circle.

 All pieces of a circle graph equal a whole.

 Each piece is a part of the circle.

Circle graphs should have a title. The title tells you what the graph is about.

 Circle graphs should have labels. The labels tell you about each part.

 Circle graphs are called pie charts. Do you know why?

Glossary

 circle graph – a graph that shows parts of a whole circle

 data – information used to create a graph

 surveys – asks a question to gather information

LERNER
SOURCE

Expand learning beyond the printed book. Download free, complementary educational resources for this book from our website, www.lerneresource.com.

Index

The images in this book are used with the permission of: © Todd Strand/Independent Picture Service, pp. 2, 3, 4, 5, 6, 7, 8, 9, 11, 14, 15, 16, 17, 18, 20, 21, 22; © Juana Arias/Washington Post/Getty Images, p. 7; © Stewart Cohen/Blend Images/Getty Images, pp. 7, 12; © Comstock Images/Getty Images, pp. 7, 10; Dean Muz/Design Pics/Newscom, pp. 7, 13.

Front cover: © Jon Fischer/Independent Picture Service.

Main body text set in ITC Avant Garde Gothic Std Medium 21/25.
Typeface provided by Adobe Systems

Lerner Publications Company
A division of Lerner Publishing Group, Inc.
241 First Avenue North
Minneapolis, MN 55401 U.S.A.

Website address: www.lernerbooks.com

Library of Congress Cataloging-in-Publication Data

Nelson, Robin, 1971–
    Let's make a circle graph / By Robin Nelson.
        p.   cm. — (First step nonfiction—graph it!)
    Includes index.
    ISBN 978–0–7613–8974–3 (lib. bdg. : alk. paper)
    1. Mathematical statistics—Graphic methods—Juvenile literature. I. Title.
    QA40.5.N454 2013
    001.4'226—dc23   2011045060

Manufactured in the United States of America
1 – BC – 7/15/12